Date: 8/20/18

**J 972.86 VAR
Vargas, Maxine,
The people and culture of
Costa Rica /**

Celebrating
Hispanic
Diversity

THE PEOPLE
AND CULTURE OF
COSTA
RICA

Maxine Vargas

PowerKiDS press.

New York

Published in 2018 by The Rosen Publishing Group, Inc.
29 East 21st Street, New York, NY 10010

First Edition

Editor: Theresa Morlock
Book Design: Rachel Rising

Photo Credits: Cover, Megapress/Alamy Stock Photo; Cover (background) John Coletti/Stockbyte/Getty Images; Cover, p. 1 https://commons.wikimedia.org/wiki/File:Flag_of_Costa_Rica_(state).svg; p. 5 iStockphotos.com/monkeybusinessimages; p. 7 Olga Gabay/Shutterstock.com; p. 9 Thornton Cohen/Alamy Stock Photo; p. 11 AFP/Stringer/Getty Images; p. 13 mbrand85/Shutterstock.com; p. 15 Omar Vega/STR/LatinContent WO/Getty Images; p. 17 S. B. Nace/Lonely Planet Images/Getty Images; p. 18 Nattika/Shutterstock.com; p. 19 adrian hepworth/Alamy Stock Photo; p. 21 https://commons.wikimedia.org/wiki/File:Teatro_Nacional_at_Night.JPG; p. 23 iStockphotos.com/Ioan Florin Cnejevici; p. 25 m.bonotto/Shutterstock.com; p. 27 Lorraine Logan/Shutterstock.com; p. 29 CP DC Press/Shutterstock.com; p. 30 Brothers Good/Shutterstock.com.

Library of Congress Cataloging-in-Publication Data

Names: Vargas, Maxine, author.
Title: The people and culture of Costa Rica / Maxine Vargas.
Description: New York : PowerKids Press, [2018] | Series: Celebrating
  Hispanic diversity | Includes index.
Identifiers: LCCN 2017023641| ISBN 9781508163121 (library bound) | ISBN
  9781538327081 (pbk.) | ISBN 9781538327524 (6 pack)
Subjects: LCSH: Costa Rica-Juvenile literature. | Costa Rica-Social life
  and customs-Juvenile literature.
Classification: LCC F1543.2 .V37 2018 | DDC 972.86–dc23
LC record available at https://lccn.loc.gov/2017023641

Manufactured in the United States of America

CPSIA Compliance Information: Batch #BW18PK: For Further Information contact Rosen Publishing, New York, New York at 1-800-237-9932

CONTENTS

A GLOBAL SOCIETY

Today, the world's population is estimated to be around 7.5 billion. This huge group is made up of people of all backgrounds—people whose **unique** cultural identities create a beautiful and **diverse** global society.

"Hispanic" is a term used to describe people who are from (or whose parents or **ancestors** came from) countries where Spanish is the main language. However, Hispanic people don't think of themselves as a single group, and there's no single Hispanic culture or identity. There are more than 20 different countries in the world whose people may identify as Hispanic. Many Hispanic people in the United States choose to identify themselves with their family's original country or area of origin. One such country is Costa Rica. The Costa Rican people are Hispanic, and their culture and traditions are very special.

Costa Rica's population is more than 4 million people. About 6 percent of those born in Costa Rica now live in another country.

Language Is Important

You may have heard people use the term "Hispanic" to describe people when they actually meant to say "Latino." These terms are often confused, but they cannot be used **interchangeably**. "Latino" is a term for a person living in the United States whose ancestors are from Latin America. Some people don't use either term to describe themselves. When someone tells you how to talk about their identity, it's important to respect that by using the language they prefer.

COSTA RICA'S GEOGRAPHY

Costa Rica is a country in Central America. It's bordered by Nicaragua to the north and Panama to the south. The country has bodies of water on two sides. The Caribbean Sea forms Costa Rica's eastern coast, and the Pacific Ocean forms its western coast.

Costa Rica is a mountainous country. Two mountain ranges run almost the length of it. There are active volcanoes in these mountains, including the country's two highest peaks: Irazú and Poás. More than half of Costa Ricans live in the Valle Central, or the highland valley.

Costa Rica receives a lot of rain, especially along its coastlines. The rainiest months in the Valle Central can see more than 12 inches (30.5 cm) of rain! Temperatures vary throughout the country, but it's generally warm, averaging about 70° Fahrenheit (21° Celsius) in San José, the country's capital.

Almost half of Costa Rica is covered by forests. Scientists believe that more than 4 percent of the world's plant and animal species can be found there.

Green, Green Lands

One color comes to mind when you think of Costa Rica: green! About one-third of Costa Rica's land is covered in forests. Throughout the lush, green land, you can find everything from the savanna oak tree to palm trees and mangroves. What lives among the trees? Monkeys, wildcats, sloths, tropical birds, snakes, iguanas, frogs, and more. Costa Rica's plant and animal life is rich and varied. This makes the country a popular place for biologists to carry out their research.

THE NATIVE PEOPLE OF COSTA RICA

Costa Rica's **indigenous** people lived in the region before Europeans arrived in the 14th century. One native people of Costa Rica were called the Chorotega. The Chorotega were the most powerful group living in Costa Rica when the Spanish arrived.

Christopher Columbus sailed to Costa Rica in 1502, and the first Spanish settlement was established in 1564. This was the village of Cartago in the Valle Central. The Spanish crown didn't invest too much time in developing Costa Rica or **conquering** it; the lands didn't have riches to claim or a large population to conquer like other Central and South American countries did.

After the Spanish arrived, the indigenous population declined significantly. Native people died of unfamiliar sicknesses brought by the Europeans. Many of those who did survive moved into the mountains to avoid Spanish rule.

Today, Costa Rica's native people make up only about 2.5 percent of the country's population.

A DEMOCRATIC SOCIETY

Costa Rica stands apart from many neighboring countries because it's considered a more politically and socially equal society. Along with other Latin American countries, Costa Rica declared independence from Spain in 1821. An early **progressive** government invested in coffee, bananas, and railroads, which helped make the country strong enough to support itself. Today, Costa Rica is a **republic**. Citizens over the age of 18 can vote in elections every four years, much like in the United States.

The Costa Rican constitution makes education free for everyone. The government invests a lot in education—almost a fourth of its budget. Ninety-five percent of Costa Rica's adult population can read and write, and its national university is one of the best schools in Central America.

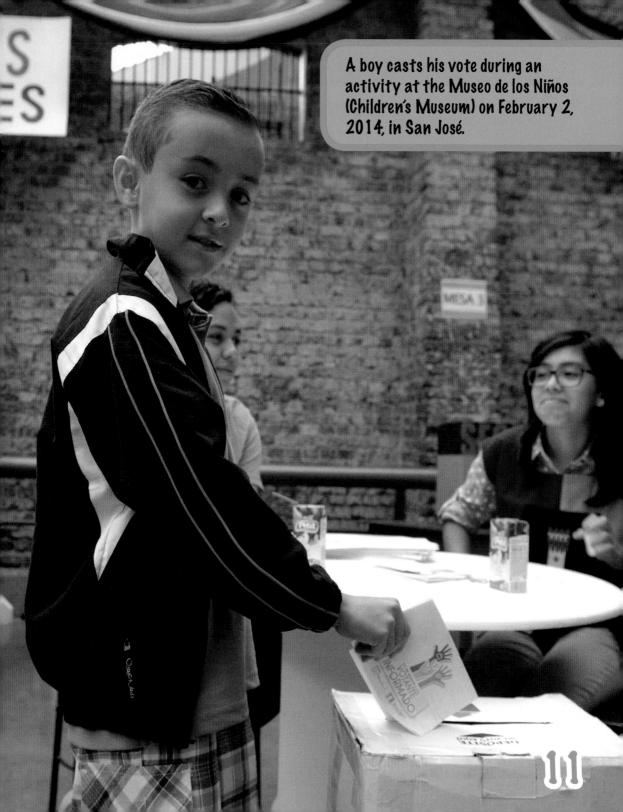

A boy casts his vote during an activity at the Museo de los Niños (Children's Museum) on February 2, 2014, in San José.

THE POPULATION OF COSTA RICA

About 80 percent of Costa Rica's population is of European and mestizo **descent**. "Mestizo" means a person has European and indigenous ancestry. A small number of people have a blend of European, indigenous, and African ancestry. Some Costa Ricans are of Chinese descent; an even smaller number of Costa Ricans are of African descent alone. A very small percent of Costa Ricans are of indigenous ancestry. Hundreds of thousands of people have immigrated to Costa Rica from the neighboring country of Nicaragua and other Central American countries.

The Valle Central is home to more than half the country's population. Most of the people there are of Spanish ancestry. Many people from the smaller populations are scattered around Costa Rica's coasts, highlands, and plains.

The city of San José is home to about one-fourth of Costa Rica's population.

In the Same Place, but Unequal

Costa Ricans with mixed ancestry are commonly the descendants of people who were brought from the West Indies in the 19th century to build the country's railroads and work on banana plantations, or large farms. Blacks were **discriminated** against through laws that limited the places where they could live and travel within the country. There were even laws that said plantation owners couldn't hire black people to work for them. While these laws were **abolished** in 1949, social prejudices still exist in Costa Rica today.

13

TICOS

Spanish is the official language in Costa Rica. Spanish explorers brought their language with them when they arrived. Spanish rulers made it the official law of the land, and Spanish has been spoken there ever since. Bribrí, Cabecar, Maléku Jaíka, Boruca, and Térraba are native languages spoken in Costa Rica.

One of the amazing things about language is that even if people are speaking the same one, it can sound different depending on where they live. For example, the Spanish spoken in Spain sounds much different than the Spanish spoken in Costa Rica. In Spanish, if you want to say something is small, it's common to add "-ito" to the end of a word. Costa Ricans and others, such as Venezuelans and Cubans, use "-ico" instead. That's why Costa Ricans are sometimes nicknamed *ticos*.

During international sporting events, such as the FIFA World Cup soccer tournament, you can hear announcers calling Costa Rica's team "The Ticos."

LIVELY HOLIDAYS

Costa Rica has a year-round calendar of holidays and festivals that give people a reason to celebrate. Many Costa Rican people are Catholic, and the country observes several religious holidays and holy days. One of the most important occasions is Semana Santa, or Holy Week. Cities and towns shut down during this holiday, which celebrates the Christian holiday Easter. Buses stop running, people are off from work, and there are many celebrations and parades to attend.

Every year in the first week of January, Costa Ricans celebrate the Fiestas Palmares. Called the country's "biggest cowboy party," it's a two-week festival of bullfighting, parades, traditional dancing, rodeos, music, and more. It's such a popular event that close to a million people attend it each year.

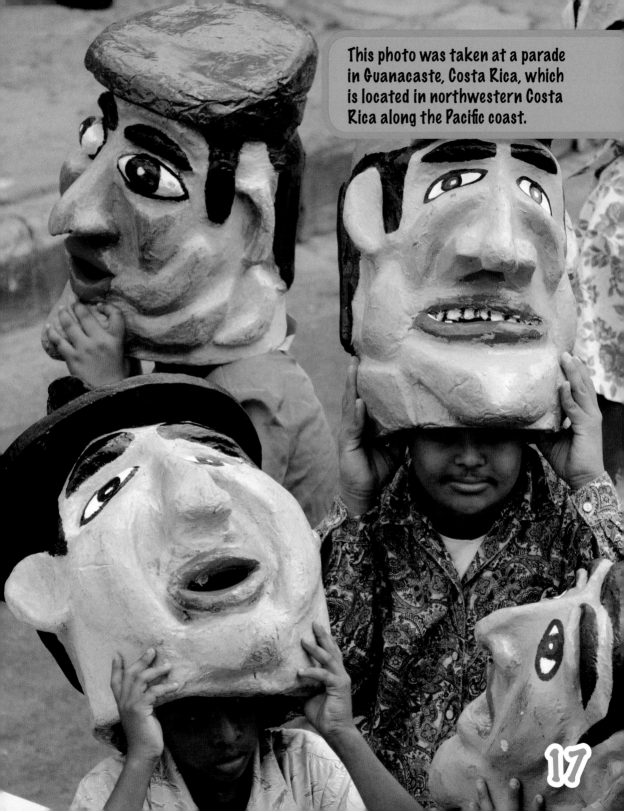

This photo was taken at a parade in Guanacaste, Costa Rica, which is located in northwestern Costa Rica along the Pacific coast.

17

CUISINE AND COFFEE CULTURE

Rice, beans, and corn play a big role in Costa Rican cooking. Casado and gallo pinto are two popular Costa Rican dishes. Casado is a type of meal with beans, rice, vegetables, meat, and other foods. Gallo pinto means "spotted rooster" in Spanish. Gallo pinto is a dish of rice and beans that are mixed together, giving it a spotted appearance. It is typically served for breakfast.

One major food product to come out of Costa Rica is something that's enjoyed around the world: coffee. The arabica coffee plant was first grown in Costa Rica in the 1700s. Coffee quickly became a huge part of the country's economy, and today Costa Rica is the world's 13th largest coffee producer. Many people consider Costa Rican coffee to be some of the best in the world.

Costa Rica's **fertile** soil, mild climate, and mountainous **terrain** provide excellent growing conditions for coffee plants.

ARTS AND LITERATURE

Costa Rica has been called a **cosmopolitan** country, which may come from the people's love of the arts. International films, live theater, music, and television are popular interests among Costa Ricans.

The National Symphony Orchestra was formed in 1971. It travels around the country to much applause. Famous Costa Rican authors include Fabián Dobles, Carlos Luis Fallas, and Carmen Naranjo.

Costa Rica's indigenous and folk art is highly prized. Large stone statues and spheres of carved stone have been found around the country. The stone spheres are believed to have decorated the houses of chiefs, but their exact purpose is unknown. Figurines made of gold and jade are treasured, too. In terms of folk art, Costa Rica is famous for its colorful, highly decorated wooden carvings and carts.

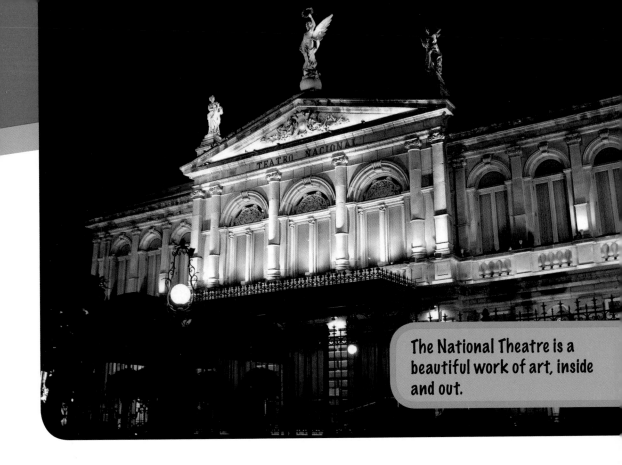

The National Theatre is a beautiful work of art, inside and out.

The National Theatre

Built in 1897, the National Theatre in San José is one of the most beautiful structures in Costa Rica. Located in the Plaza of Culture, the National Theatre has statues, staircases made of marble, and famous ceiling murals in the second vestibule. One of them honors Costa Rica's coffee and banana growers, key to the country's economy. Today, Costa Ricans and visitors attend the National Theatre to see musical performances and live theater.

21

TRADITIONAL CLOTHING

Clothing can reveal a lot about a society. It can show how people deal with their climate, the social differences between men and women, and other important things, such as religious beliefs. Clothing styles and trends can spread from one area to another. So today, many countries share the same style of dress.

Costa Ricans dress in Western-style clothing. They wear the same jeans, pants, T-shirts, and sweaters you probably see in your city or town. However, traditional clothing looks quite different. Men may wear long pants, a white shirt, and a sash. Women wear a long skirt made with layers of color and a ruffled white top. This kind of clothing is worn for festivals and holidays when people perform traditional folk dances.

Traditional costumes are different in each province. This one is from the province of Limón, in eastern Costa Rica.

MUSIC, NEW AND OLD

The northwest province of Costa Rica is Guanacaste, and it's from this region that Costa Rica's most well-known folk music traditions come. Folk music is traditional music of an area that's passed down over generations. Costa Ricans use two special instruments in their folk music: the ocarina and the marimba.

An ocarina is a wind instrument that's often shaped like a potato but some resemble animals. It has a mouthpiece and small finger holes used to make different notes. The Costa Rican ocarina is called a *dru mugata*, and it's different from most ocarinas because it's made of beeswax. The marimba is a percussion instrument. The player hits wooden keys with large mallets to produce notes. Three people at a time can play a large marimba! They can create beautiful rhythms for dancing.

COSTA RICAN OCARINA

Listening to a culture's music is a great way to learn about its people. Common musical themes in Costa Rican music include love and patriotism.

THE ART OF DANCING

Dancing is a popular activity in Costa Rica. Dance halls and clubs called discotheques—or discos— are common in San José. On weekend nights, the clubs are full of *ticos* looking to dance the night away! Dance halls play everything from today's popular music to traditional Latin music such as salsa, merengue, and bachata.

Folk dancing is a way for Costa Ricans to celebrate their heritage. The Guancaste region is the heart of traditional Costa Rican dancing. A performance is quite something to see. While musicians keep time with guitars, *dru mugata*, marimbas, and more, dancers in traditional costumes perform with flair and style. Dancers spin in their large skirts and wave scarves, telling stories of love and tradition to their audience.

Folk dances are usually performed for holidays, tourists, and festivals.

27

FOR THE LOVE OF THE GAME

Sports are a big part of many cultures. The love of sports can unite a country as fans take much pride in their teams' success. The most popular sport in Costa Rica is football, or *fútbol*, which we call soccer in the United States. There are dozens of football clubs and regional teams throughout Costa Rica.

Football was introduced to Costa Rica in the 1900s. Today, Ticos play a style of the game that's been called aggressive. This may be why their national team is the most successful in the history of Central America. Nicknamed La Sele, La Tricolor, and the Ticos, Costa Rica's national team has won eight championships as of 2016. Other popular activities include bullfighting, surfing, fishing, and other nature sports.

A Land of Adventure

Costa Rica is often thought of as a place of adventure, especially for visitors to the country. This may be because of the beautiful landscapes, which offer plenty of fun sports on land and in the water. Surfing, swimming, and fishing in the country's crystal-clear waters are popular activities. Zip-lining through the Costa Rican rain forests is an adventure many tourists like to experience. Mountain biking and rafting are popular activities, too.

A CHANGING CULTURAL IDENTITY

When people **immigrate** to a different country, they bring their traditions and heritage with them. Today, there are about 140,000 Costa Rican Americans, half of whom were born in the United States. Costa Rican Americans make up about 0.3 percent of the total Hispanic population of the United States. Costa Rican immigrants to the United States share their rich cultural traditions with the people of their new home, making valuable contributions to the varied cultural landscape of the country.

Embracing new traditions and celebrating old ones is a way to keep cultural identities alive—something very important in our increasingly diverse world. Costa Rican culture continues to change and grow with its people. The result is a country rich in Hispanic tradition.

GLOSSARY

abolish: To officially end or stop something.

ancestor: Somebody who comes before others in their family tree.

conquer: To take over.

cosmopolitan: Familiar and at ease with different cultures.

descent: The background of a person in terms of their family or nationality.

discriminate: To treat people unequally based on class, race, religion, or another factor.

diverse: Made up of things that are different from each other.

fertile: Capable of growing many healthy crops.

immigrate: To come to a country to live there.

indigenous: The first people of an area.

interchangeable: Able to be used in place of each other.

progressive: Interested in or using new or modern ideas.

republic: A form of government in which the people elect representatives who run the government.

terrain: A type of land in an area.

unique: Special or different from anything else.

INDEX

WEBSITES

Due to the changing nature of Internet links, PowerKids Press has developed an online list of websites related to the subject of this book. This site is updated regularly. Please use this link to access the list: www.powerkidslinks.com/chd/costa